EXPRESS YOURSELF

In Written English

Frederick H. O'Connor

National Textbook Company
a division of *NTC Publishing Group* • Lincolnwood, Illinois USA

About the Author

Frederick O'Connor received an M.A.T. from the School for International Training in Brattleboro, Vermont. He has taught English language skills in the United States, Japan, Afghanistan, and Iran. Currently, he is an instructor at the Intensive American Language Center at Washington State University.

1997 Printing

Published by National Textbook Company, a division of NTC Publishing Group.
© 1990 by NTC Publishing Group, 4255 West Touhy Avenue,
Lincolnwood (Chicago), Illinois 60646-1975 U.S.A.

7 8 9 0 VP 9 8 7

CONTENTS

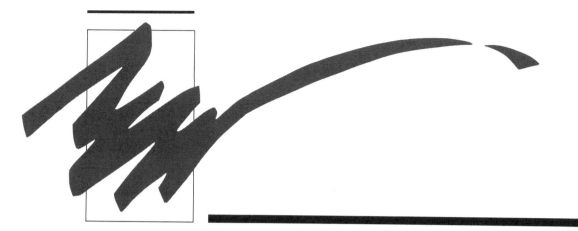

Introduction

Express Yourself in Written English develops the expository writing skills that young adult and adult students need to express their ideas clearly and concisely. Through highly illustrative examples and carefully structured questions and directions, students complete, step by step, activities that enable them to understand and fully participate in the writing process.

The effective workbook/textbook format provides students with a powerful four-step approach to paragraph and composition writing. Students will accomplish the following writing tasks that lead to clear and concise paragraphs and compositions:

Exposure: the initial step, in which students read a model paragraph or composition.

Analysis: the second step, in which students gain greater understanding of the structure of the model through directed questions and guided activities.

Planning: the third step, in which students outline original paragraphs or compositions based on their understanding of the models.

Writing: the final step, in which students write original full paragraphs or compositions.

Students focus on the content and style of expository writing as they complete each of the four steps for the paragraphs and multiparagraph compositions that they compose. Students will master fundamentals of effective single paragraph composition such as paragraph layout, central idea, topic sentence, body of the paragraph, and paragraph conclusion. They will also become familiar with the forms and functions of outlines; develop their own useful outlines; and plan and write multiparagraph compositions.

The book is divided into two units. In Unit One, students work with single paragraph compositions including simple listing paragraphs, order of importance paragraphs, time order paragraphs, and spatial order paragraphs. In Unit Two, students will read and write compositions with several paragraphs including contrastive compositions and cause and effect compositions.

Throughout *Express Yourself in Written English* students are encouraged to write about topics that interest them and are motivated to become fully engaged in the writing process as they express their ideas and develop effective techniques for clear and concise written communication.

PART I

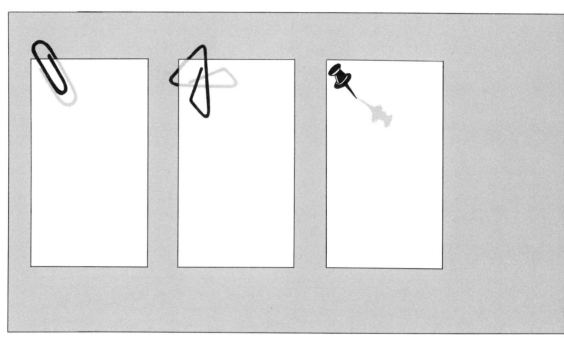

Single Paragraph Compositions

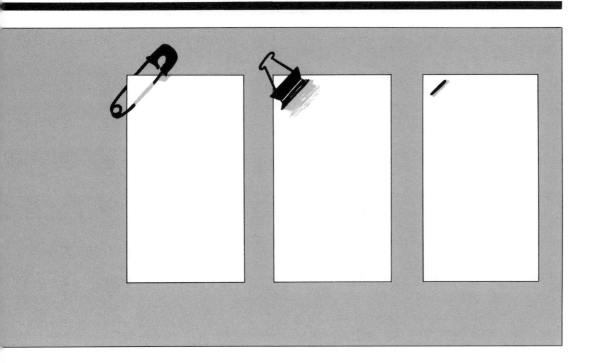

In Units 1–4, you will read and write

- **simple listing paragraphs**
- **order of importance paragraphs**
- **time order paragraphs**
- **spatial order paragraphs**

UNIT 1

Simple Listing Paragraphs

1.1 This is a list:

water bottle
sweater
compass
sandwiches
camera

This is also a list:

I need a water bottle for the hike in case I get thirsty.
A sweater is useful if it gets cold.
A compass will help me go in the right direction.
Sandwiches will be an easy-to-carry snack.
I can use a camera to take pictures of unusual or attractive places.

1.2 Is the following a *list* or a *paragraph*?

I need a water bottle for the hike in case I get thirsty. A sweater is useful if it gets cold. A compass will help me go in the right direction. Sandwiches will be an easy-to-carry snack. I can use a camera to take pictures of unusual or attractive places.

It is *not* a paragraph.
It is in *paragraph form* because it begins with an indent.

Even though it is in paragraph form, it is not a paragraph.

1.3 Why isn't it a paragraph?

It isn't a paragraph because it has no *central idea*. Without a central idea, a group of sentences is just a list, and not an actual paragraph.

1.4   Can we make it a paragraph?
Yes, we can.
How can we make it a paragraph?
We can make it a paragraph by giving it a *central idea,* or a focus.
How do we give it a focus?
We give it a focus by stating the central idea of the paragraph in one sentence.
What is this sentence called?
It is called the *topic sentence.* The topic sentence is usually found at the beginning of the paragraph.

1.5   Let's look at the sentences again:

    I need a water bottle for the hike in case I get thirsty. A sweater is useful if it gets cold. A compass will help me go in the right direction. Sandwiches will be an easy-to-carry snack. I can use a camera to take pictures of unusual or attractive places.

1.6   Let's try to supply a central idea for the sentences. All the sentences tell about things needed for a hike. *In a few words*, write a central idea for these sentences. (You do not need to write a complete sentence.)

_____

_____

Be sure that your central idea covers all of the ideas in the sentences. Now write a complete sentence containing the central idea. This is your topic sentence.

_____

_____

1.7   Now write your first paragraph. First write your topic sentence, and then write the sentences from 1.5. Be sure to indent your paragraph.

_____

_____

_____

_____

_____

_____

1.8   Before we can call this a *complete paragraph*, we must add one more sentence. This sentence is called the conclusion. It comes at the end of the paragraph, and it makes the reader feel the paragraph is complete.

From the three choices below, choose the best conclusion for the paragraph you wrote in 1.7.

1. My water bottle is the heaviest.
2. I need many items to be ready for a safe, enjoyable hike.
3. I have never camped overnight in a tent.

Which did you choose? _____

1.9   The correct answer is 2 because 2 works best to tie all the ideas in the paragraph together and to make the reader feel that the paragraph is complete.

Now try to write a conclusion for the paragraph that is better than "I need many items to be ready for a safe, enjoyable hike." First, in a few words, write your idea for the conclusion.

_____

_____

Now write a complete sentence that expresses the idea.

_____

_____

Now you can write a complete English paragraph. First, write your topic sentence. Then write the sentences from 1.5. Finally, write your conclusion. Be sure to indent your paragraph.

_____

_____

_____

_____

_____

1.10   The kind of paragraph you just wrote is called a *simple listing* paragraph.

1.11 Now write a simple listing paragraph of your own. Choose one central idea from the list below.

- my courses at school
- my favorite things
- my favorite people
- the people in my family

First write the central idea you chose and add something that makes that central idea more focused.
Example: my favorite things = my favorite things to do in summer

_____

_____

Now make a list of those people or things and write some information about each one.

people/things   **information**

1. _____   _____
                            _____

2. _____   _____
                            _____

3. _____   _____
                            _____

4. _____   _____
                            _____

Now write an idea for your conclusion.

_____

1.12 Now you will write a paragraph based on the ideas you outlined in 1.11. First, write a sentence containing your central idea. Next, write one sentence for each person or thing on your list. (This is called the _body_ of the paragraph.) Finally, write a sentence for your conclusion.

_____

_____

_____

_____

_____

1.13   **Let's review.**

What does every good paragraph have?

1. _____

2. _____

3. _____

1.14   **Read the paragraph below.**

New York City has many interesting areas. Chinatown is a neighborhood where you can eat good Chinese food. On Fifth Avenue, you can see many beautiful stores. Greenwich Village has interesting clubs and restaurants. Broadway is the center of American theater. Truly, New York has something for everyone.

1.15   **In a few words, write the central idea of the paragraph in 1.14.**

_____

_____

_____

Now list each item mentioned in the paragraph and what was said about it.

item	what was said
_____	_____
_____	_____
_____	_____
_____	_____

Now write the idea for the conclusion.

_____

_____

1.16   Next you will outline a paragraph similar to the one in 1.14. In your paragraph, you should describe a place or an area you know well, say what is there, and give some details about what is there. In your outline, write your ideas, using only a few words. *Do not* write in full sentences.

Central idea _____

Body

item   information

_____   _____

_____   _____

_____   _____

_____   _____

_____   _____

Conclusion _____

_____

_____

1.17   Now, writing a sentence for each item above, write your paragraph.

_____

_____

_____

_____

_____

_____

_____

_____

_____

_____

1.18 Here's another simple listing paragraph.

There are many ways to improve your tennis game. You can work to increase your overall strength and stamina by running or doing other exercises. You might engage in other games that require quick reflexes and reactions, such as handball. Or you could work directly on your tennis game by taking lessons to improve your weak points. More passively, you can read books on tennis to understand the strategy of the game better. No matter which way you choose to reach your goal, you should work at it regularly over a period of time.

1.19 Now outline the paragraph in 1.18.

Central idea _____

Body

item   information

_____   _____

                                       _____

_____   _____

                                       _____

_____   _____

                                       _____

_____   _____

                                       _____

Conclusion _____

1.20 Next you will write a similar paragraph telling someone how to improve at something like a sport, a game, an art, or a hobby. First outline your ideas.

Central idea _____

Body

item   information

_____   _____

                                  _____

_____   _____

                                  _____

_____   _____

                                  _____

                                  _____

_____   _____

                                  _____

Conclusion _____

_____

1.21 Now write your paragraph. You may want to use more than one sentence for the central idea, each item, or the conclusion.

_____

_____

_____

_____

_____

_____

_____

_____

_____

_____

1.22   *FREE PRACTICE*

Write a simple listing paragraph on any topic you like.

First outline your ideas.

Central idea _____

Body

item	information
_____	_____
	_____
_____	_____
	_____
_____	_____
	_____
_____	_____
	_____

Conclusion _____

Now complete your paragraph.

_____

_____

_____

_____

_____

_____

_____

_____

_____

_____

_____

UNIT 2

Order of Importance Paragraphs

2.1 The *order of importance paragraph* has all the elements of the simple listing paragraph. It has an *introduction*, a *body*, and a *conclusion*. The difference between these two kinds of paragraphs is in the body.

2.2 Read these two paragraphs.

1

When we choose a car, we must think about many things. It must be big enough for the number of people we want to carry. It must not cost more than we want to spend. It should be fuel efficient. We want a car that looks good. It can be difficult to find the right car.

2

When we choose a car, we must think about many things. The most important is that it must be big enough for the number of people we want to carry. The second most important thing is that it must not cost more than we want to spend. Third, it should be fuel efficient. Last, we want a car that looks good. It can be difficult to find the right car.

2.3 What's the difference between these paragraphs?

Paragraph 1 is a simple listing paragraph. It simply lists the things we must think about when we buy a car.

Paragraph 2 also lists the things we must think about when we buy a car, *but* it lists them in their order of importance. It lists them in the order from most important to least important.

2.4 Look at paragraph 2 again. Below, on the right are listed the important things. On the left, write the words from paragraph 2 that tell you which is most important, second most important, third most important, and fourth most important.

_____	**big enough**
_____	**not cost too much**
_____	**fuel efficient**
_____	**good-looking**

2.5 **Refer again to paragraph 2 in 2.2.**

What is the central idea? _____

What is the conclusion? _____

2.6 **To help you understand the structure of this paragraph, read it in the form below.**

Central idea	When we choose a car, we must think about many things.
Most important idea	The most important is that it must be big enough for the number of people we want to carry.
2nd idea	The second most important thing is that it must not cost more than we want to spend.
3rd idea	Third, it should be fuel efficient.
4th idea	Last, we want a car that looks good.
Conclusion	It can be difficult to find the right car.

2.7 **Let's review.**

What's the difference between a simple listing paragraph and an order of importance paragraph?

In a simple listing paragraph, the items are not listed in any order.

In an order of importance paragraph, the items are listed in an order.

Does this necessarily have to be an order of *importance?*

No, it doesn't. It could be

order of importance   OR
order of interest   OR
order of difficulty

List any other kinds of order you can think of.

order of _____

order of _____

2.8   Read the paragraph below.

What Makes a Good Boss

There are three important qualities necessary in a good boss. The most important is fairness. If the boss is fair, workers can feel that if they do a good job, their work will be appreciated, and their efforts will be rewarded. The second most important quality is leadership. The boss should be an example and a teacher. This allows workers to learn from a boss so that they can increase their job skills and get promoted. The third most important factor is that the boss acts with consistency. That way the workers know what to expect each day. They know how they'll be treated and what their share of the workload will be. I would hire a boss with these qualities for myself.

2.9   Now outline "What Makes a Good Boss" from 2.8.

Central idea _____

Body

	idea	why it's important

Most
important   _____   _____

                                _____

2nd most
important   _____   _____

                                _____

3rd most
important   _____   _____

                                _____

Conclusion _____

2.10   Outline your own paragraph on the three most important factors in choosing the right job.

Central idea _____

Body

	idea	why it's important
Most important	_____	_____
2nd most important	_____	_____
3rd most important	_____	_____

Conclusion _____

2.11   Now choose a title for your paragraph. The purpose of the title is to catch the interest of the reader and make him or her interested in what you have written. Think about interesting movie, play, or book titles that caught your interest. Think about what qualities made them interesting to you. Try to write an original title.

_____

2.12   Now write your composition. First, write the title. Second, write a sentence for the central idea. Third, write *at least* one sentence for each other idea. Last, write a sentence for your conclusion.

_____

_____

_____

_____

_____

_____

_____

_____

2.13 **Now read another order of importance paragraph.**

America's Three Biggest Cities

Chicago, Los Angeles, and New York City are the three largest
cities in the United States. Among them, they contain more than 20
percent of America's population. Chicago, the smallest of the three
with a population of about 3 million, is in the state of Illinois in the
nation's Midwest. Its largest industries are the transportation and
metal industries. It is famous for its modern architecture—
particularly its skyscrapers. Los Angeles, the second-largest city, is in
California and has a population of slightly over 3 million. It is famous
for Hollywood, the movie-making capital of America. It is also well
known for its sprawling highways. New York, America's largest city,
has a population of about 7 million. It is America's largest port and is
the nation's financial center. With its many theaters, museums, and
ballet companies, it is first in cultural activities. Each city is a typical
large American city—but each has its own "personality" and
qualities.

2.14 **Now outline "America's Three Biggest Cities" from 2.13.**

Central idea _____

Body
3rd
largest   _____   _____

                                _____

                                _____

2nd
largest   _____   _____

                                _____

                                _____

Largest   _____   _____

                                _____

                                _____

Conclusion _____

2.15   **Now write a *full* outline of a paragraph on one of the following:**

- the three biggest cities in your area or country
- the three most important historical places in your area or country
- the three most interesting places in your hometown

Central idea _____

Body

3rd   _____   _____

                                   _____

2nd   _____   _____

                                   _____

1st   _____   _____

                                   _____

Conclusion _____

Title _____

2.16   **Now write a paragraph based on your outline in 2.15.**

                    _____

_____

_____

_____

_____

_____

_____

_____

_____

_____

_____

_____

2.17 **Read the following order of importance paragraph.**

Two Essential Courses

Although I know that I have to study a variety of subjects to become a well-rounded person, there are two courses on which I put special focus. The most important course to me is math. The reason for my attitude comes from my career plans: I want to work designing computer programs. Mathematics, of course, is basic to understanding computer operations. The course that is second in importance to me is English. In computer design, as in any business area, it is important to be able to communicate correctly and effectively. English will give me the tools to express my ideas and to write effective memos and letters. By working particularly hard in these classes, I feel I am furthering my career plans, as well as getting good grades now!

2.18 **Now outline "Two Essential Courses" from 2.17.**

Central idea _____

_____

Body

	idea	why it's important
Most important	_____	_____
		_____
		_____
2nd most important	_____	_____
		_____
		_____

Conclusion _____

_____

_____

2.19 **Outline your own paragraph on the three most interesting activities you do outside of school.**

Central idea _____

Body

	idea	why it's important
Most important	_____	_____
		_____
		_____
2nd most important	_____	_____
		_____
		_____
3rd most important	_____	_____
		_____
		_____

Conclusion _____

_____

Title _____

_____

2.20   Now write a composition based on your outline in 2.19.

_____

_____

_____

_____

_____

_____

_____

_____

_____

_____

_____

_____

_____

_____

_____

_____

_____

_____

_____

_____

_____

_____

_____

2.21   *FREE PRACTICE*

Write an order of importance paragraph about one of the following:

- the three movies you like best
- the three books you like best
- the three musicians you like best
- your three favorite _____

First outline your ideas.

Central idea _____

_____

Body
1st   _____   _____

                           _____

                           _____

2nd   _____   _____

                           _____

                           _____

3rd   _____   _____

                           _____

                           _____

Conclusion _____

_____

Title _____

_____

2.22   Now write a paragraph based on your outline in 2.21.

UNIT 3

Time Order Paragraphs

3.1   We use *time order paragraphs* to describe a series of events in the order in which the events happened. Time order paragraphs list events *sequentially*. Time order is mostly used to tell a story. This can be a personal story or a history.

3.2   Read this paragraph.

My European Holiday

Last year I took a month-long trip to Europe. First, I went to London. I stayed there for two weeks. I saw many historical places and went to several shows. After London, I flew to Paris, where I went shopping and visited the Louvre. I stayed in Paris for a week. Then I went to Rome by train. In Rome I saw the Colosseum, the Pantheon, and Vatican City. After a week in Rome, I flew home. It was an educational and enjoyable trip.

3.3   What is the central idea of "My European Holiday" in 3.2?

_____

Write the *words* that tell you the *time order* of the events.

went to London   _____

went to Paris   _____

went to Rome   _____

returned home   _____

What is the idea of the conclusion?

_____

As you can see, the time order paragraph also has the three elements of any good paragraph: an introduction that expresses the central idea, a body, and a conclusion.

3.4 **To help you understand the structure of the paragraph, read the body in the following form.**

Introduction: Last year I took a month-long trip to Europe.

Body:

- First, I went to London. I stayed there for two weeks. I saw many historical places and went to several shows.
- After London, I flew to Paris, where I went shopping and visited the Louvre. I stayed in Paris for a week.
- Then I went to Rome by train. In Rome, I saw the Colosseum, the Pantheon, and Vatican City.
- After a week in Rome, I flew home.

→ **Time** →

Conclusion: It was an educational and enjoyable trip.

3.5 **Write a time order paragraph telling what you did on a trip.**

Central idea _____

Body

time words	what you did
_____	_____
	_____
_____	_____
	_____
_____	_____
	_____

Conclusion _____

Title _____

3.6   Now write a paragraph based on your outline in 3.5.

_____

_____

_____

_____

_____

_____

_____

3.7   Here's another time order paragraph.

Putting on Our Play

Last weekend we put on our annual drama club play. It was a great success, but it was also hard work. We began planning two months ago. First, we selected the play. Next, a director was chosen. After that, we began casting the play. The next step was to find people to design and make the costumes and sets. All this while, we were rehearsing. Finally, two weeks ago, we held a dress rehearsal, and, at last, we felt we were ready for opening night. Because of all our hard work and careful preparations, the play was a big hit.

3.8   Now outline the ideas in 3.7.

Central idea _____

Body

time words	what happened
------------------------------	---
------------------------------	---
------------------------------	---
------------------------------	---
------------------------------	---
------------------------------	---
------------------------------	---

Conclusion _____

3.9 Now write an outline of a paragraph describing the planning of a group event or activity.

Central idea _____

Body

time words	what happened
-----------------------------	---
-----------------------------	---
-----------------------------	---
-----------------------------	---
-----------------------------	---
-----------------------------	---
-----------------------------	---

Conclusion _____

Title _____

3.10 Write a paragraph based on your outline in 3.9.

_____

_____

_____

_____

_____

_____

_____

_____

_____

_____

_____

3.11 Read this time order paragraph.

City or Country?

I was born in 1969 in New York City. I lived there until 1979, when I was ten. That year my father got a new job, and we moved to rural Vermont. At first I didn't like living in the country because I had never lived outside New York City before. Eventually, I got to like it very much. When I graduated from high school in 1988, I had a big decision to make: Should I go to college in the city or in the country? I thought about it for a long time, and, finally, I decided to stay in the country. In the autumn of 1988, I enrolled in the University of Vermont, where I'm now in my junior year. I'm very happy about the choice I made. When I finish college, I'd like to find a job—in the country.

3.12 Outline the paragraph in 3.11 by writing the events next to the time line below.

Central idea _____

_____

Body

T

I

M

E

Conclusion _____

3.13　**Now use the time line below to outline a paragraph about one memorable period in your life: for example, a memorable summer or your first months in a new situation.**

Central Idea _____

Body

T

I

M

E

Conclusion _____

Title _____

3.14　**Now write a paragraph based on your outline in 3.13.**

_____

_____

_____

_____

_____

_____

_____

_____

_____

3.15   The time order paragraph below tells the history of an organization.

International College

International College, where I am a student, is located in the suburbs of Chicago. It was founded in 1946 by Francis Williams, a former ambassador, and was originally known as the European Language Institute. For the first fourteen years it was in existence, it was a school for training teachers of foreign languages; the languages offered were French, Spanish, Italian, and German. In 1960 the school broadened its educational program to include politics, as the Department of International Relations was formed. In that year, the school's name was changed to International College. The Department of International Commerce came into existence in 1965, and the Department of International Law was started in 1969. At present the school has more than 700 students and a faculty of 42. In the past twenty years, the school has gained a good reputation for training young people for careers in education, government, and business.

3.16   Now outline the paragraph in 3.15.

Central idea _____

Introduction _____

Body

T

I

M

E

Conclusion _____

_____

3.17   **Now outline your own paragraph on the history of an organization you know well.**

Central idea _____

Introduction _____

Body

T

I

M

E

Conclusion _____

Title _____

3.18   **Now write a paragraph based on your outline in 3.17.**

_____

_____

_____

_____

_____

_____

_____

_____

_____

_____

_____

_____

3.19   Read this story, which is told in a time order paragraph.

A Brave Girl

Once there was a young girl named Nari who lived with her parents near the banks of a large river. Nari's father always warned her to stay away from the river. There were strong currents in the river that could drown even a strong swimmer. One day Nari was playing by the river. Even though her father had warned her about the danger, Nari still found the river fascinating. As she was playing, she heard a shout. A little boy was in the water, holding on to a piece of wood that was floating in the current. He looked scared. Without thinking of her own safety, Nari jumped into the water to help the boy. She swam out to him and grabbed hold of the piece of wood, but no matter how hard she tried, she couldn't get to the shore. After they had floated quite a way, they came to a bend in the river where a tree hung out over the water. Nari grabbed the boy with one hand and a tree branch with the other. Using all of her strength, she pulled herself and the boy out of the water. Just then her father came along the path next to the river. Although Nari had disobeyed him, her father could not be angry with her. He was too proud of what his daughter had done.

3.20   Now outline "A Brave Girl" from 3.19.

Central idea _____

Introduction _____

_____

Body

time words	what happened
----------------------------	--
----------------------------	--
----------------------------	--
----------------------------	--
----------------------------	--
----------------------------	--
----------------------------	--

Conclusion _____

3.21   Now outline a time order paragraph to tell a story you know. This story can be from a TV show or a movie. It could be a fairy tale or a folk story.

Central idea _____

Introduction _____

Body

time words	what happened
----------------------------	--
----------------------------	--
----------------------------	--
----------------------------	--
----------------------------	--
----------------------------	--
----------------------------	--
----------------------------	--

Conclusion _____

Title _____

3.22   Now write a paragraph based on your outline in 3.21.

_____

_____

_____

_____

_____

_____

_____

_____

3.23 Read this time order paragraph.

Miscommunication

Sometimes making a mistake doesn't have such terrible consequences, as an experience I had in Italy has proved to me. I had been wanting to stay in a hotel with a view in Florence for a long time, and finally it seemed my wish was going to come true. I had reserved a room in a hotel along the Arno River before leaving home. On my arrival I was disappointed to get a room without a view—but with mosquitoes. Throughout the night, just as I was dozing off, the mosquitoes buzzed around my head. The next morning I went to the hotel office to report the problem and to say that my sleep had been disturbed the night before. I figured I might have to look for another hotel. As I was attempting to communicate in my just-above-basic Italian, I suddenly realized I had said "gypsies" were in my room, not "mosquitoes," the two words being somewhat similar. The clerk first looked at me in surprise, and then as I was correcting myself, he smiled and became quite friendly. The result was that the clerk offered to change my room. I ended up with a room with a view and without mosquitoes. Miscommunication sometimes can have positive results.

3.24 Using the time line below, outline "Miscommunication" from 3.23.

Central idea _____

Introduction _____

_____

Body

Conclusion _____

_____

3.25 Now prepare an outline for your own paragraph telling of a language or cultural misunderstanding you have experienced. Be sure to tell what you learned from that experience.

Central idea _____

Introduction _____

_____

Body

T

I

M

E

Conclusion _____

Title _____

3.26 Write a paragraph based on your outline in 3.25.

_____

_____

_____

_____

_____

_____

_____

_____

_____

_____

_____

3.27 FREE PRACTICE

Prepare an outline for a paragraph in which you tell the story of a book you have read or a movie you have seen.

Central idea/Introduction _____

_____

_____

Body

time words	what happened
------------------------------	--
------------------------------	--
------------------------------	--
------------------------------	--
------------------------------	--
------------------------------	--
------------------------------	--
------------------------------	--

Conclusion _____

Title _____

Now write your paragraph.

_____

_____

_____

_____

_____

_____

_____

UNIT 4

Spatial Order Paragraphs

4.1 **A *spatial order paragraph* describes a scene.**

4.2 **Read the paragraph below.**

A Comfortable Place

My favorite room is my living room. It's rectangular with the door
on the left side of the south wall. In the wall opposite the door is a
picture window. Below the window is a sofa. A rectangular coffee
table is in front of the sofa. Facing the sofa are two armchairs. An
abstract painting is on the west wall. Along the east wall you will see
a long cabinet with a vase of flowers on it. To the right of the cabinet
is a small table with a telephone on it. This bright and uncluttered
room is my favorite place to relax.

4.3 **Fill in this diagram, using the description in 4.2.**

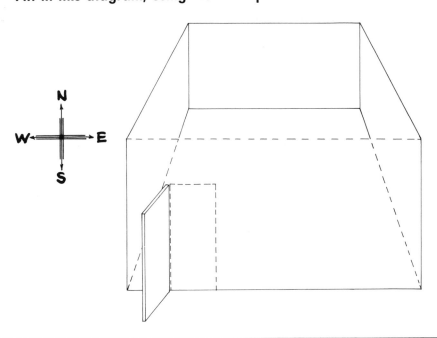

4.4   Look carefully at this picture of a library room.

4.5   Divide the room in 4.4 into five sections: front, back, left, right, and center. In the outline below, write the section names on the left in the order in which you plan to describe them. Then write the names of the item(s) in each section in the middle, and the words to describe the location of each item on the right.

section	item	words to describe location

4.6   **Before writing a paragraph based on your outline in 4.5, you must choose an idea for the introduction, an idea for the conclusion, and a title for your paragraph.**

Central idea _____

Conclusion _____

Title _____

Now you are ready to write your paragraph.

_____

_____

_____

_____

_____

_____

_____

_____

_____

_____

_____

_____

_____

_____

_____

_____

_____

_____

_____

4.7   Draw a diagram of a room you know well.

4.8   Now divide the room into sections. Write the section names on the left *in the order in which you plan to describe the sections.* Then complete the outline by listing the item(s) in each section and the location word(s) for each item.

section	item	words to describe location
	_____	_____
	_____	_____
	_____	_____
	_____	_____
	_____	_____
	_____	_____
	_____	_____
	_____	_____

Central idea _____

Conclusion _____

Title _____

4.9 **Now write a paragraph based on your outline in 4.8. First, give the central idea in your topic sentence. After that, describe each item in the room. Finally, write the conclusion.**

4.10　Read this spatial order paragraph.

Our Campus

The campus of International College is on the north side of Route 107 in suburban Overston. It's a rectangular piece of land about two miles from east to west and one mile from north to south. One long side of the rectangle fronts on Route 107. In the center of this side is the main entrance. Directly inside the main entrance is the Administration Building. It's a three-story brick building, the oldest building on campus. It contains the administrators' and teachers' offices. To the east of the Administration Building is the Classroom Building. It's a long, two-story building, with the long side facing the Administration Building. To the west of the Administration Building are four dormitories arranged in a square. Directly behind the Administration Building is the Student Center. It's our newest building and has a cafeteria, lounge, and activity rooms. It's a one-story circular building. To the north of the Student Center is the gymnasium. It's quite small, and we're hoping to build a new one next year. Behind the gymnasium are the playing fields. We have a soccer field, a baseball diamond, and a football field. They run side by side from east to west on the north side of the campus. Our campus is not very big, but it has everything we need. It's a small, but comfortable, place to study.

4.11　Draw a diagram of the campus of International College as it is described in 4.10. Be sure to include Route 107, all the buildings mentioned, and the playing fields.

4.12 Draw a diagram of your school or university campus. If the area is very big, you may want to draw only a part of it. If your school is just one building, you may want to include places near the school.

4.13 Now outline a paragraph based on your diagram in 4.12. Be sure to list the items *in the order in which you plan to describe them.*

Location _____

Size and Shape _____

item   **words to describe location**

_____   _____

_____   _____

_____   _____

_____   _____

_____   _____

_____   _____

Conclusion _____

Title _____

4.14   **Write a paragraph based on your outline in 4.13.**

_____

_____

_____

_____

_____

_____

_____

_____

_____

_____

_____

_____

_____

_____

_____

_____

_____

_____

_____

_____

_____

4.15   Look at this map.

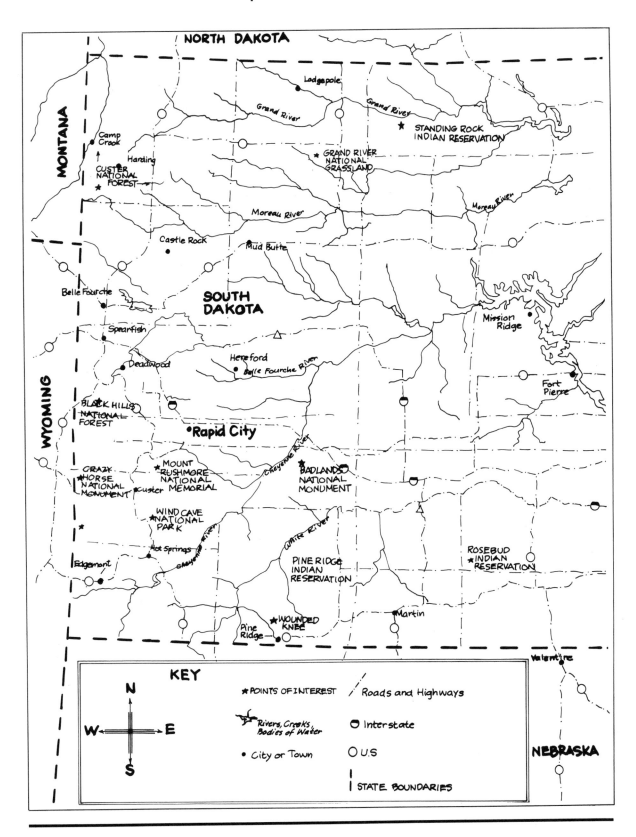

4.16   Now read the description

The Black Hills Region

In the southwestern corner of the state of South Dakota in the United States is the Black Hills region, one of the most visited areas of the West. The Belle Fourche and Cheyenne rivers bound the region, both flowing northeast to join the Missouri River. The chief city of the area is Rapid City, at the eastern edge of the Black Hills. To the southwest of the city is the famous site, Mount Rushmore. Here the heads of four presidents are carved into a hill. Another unusual place is Wind Cave National Park, almost directly south of Mount Rushmore. The cave is named from the wind that rushes in and out of it to produce a strange noise. To the southwest of Rapid City is Crazy Horse Monument, a gigantic sculpture of a famous native American Indian chief. All these attractions and the beautiful mountains make the Black Hills an important tourist area.

4.17   List the words that tell the location of each place.

Black Hills _____

Rapid City _____

Mount Rushmore _____

Wind Cave National Park _____

Crazy Horse Monument _____

4.18 **Now use the space below to draw a map of a place you know well.**

4.19 Complete the following outline for a paragraph describing your drawing in 4.18. List each of the items on your map on the left in the order in which you plan to describe them. On the right, write the words that will tell where they are.

item   location words

_____   _____

_____   _____

_____   _____

_____   _____

_____   _____

_____   _____

_____   _____

Central idea _____

Conclusion _____

Title _____

4.20   Now write a paragraph based on your outline in 4.19. Try to refer only to 4.19, and not to your map in 4.18. You may want to add some information about the places you are describing.

4.21 *FREE PRACTICE*

Picture in your mind a place that you know very well. Now write an outline of a paragraph describing that place without drawing a diagram first.

item   location words

_____   _____

_____   _____

_____   _____

_____   _____

_____   _____

_____   _____

_____   _____

_____   _____

Central idea _____

Conclusion _____

Title _____

4.22 **Now write your paragraph.**

_____

_____

_____

_____

_____

_____

_____

_____

_____

_____

_____

PART II

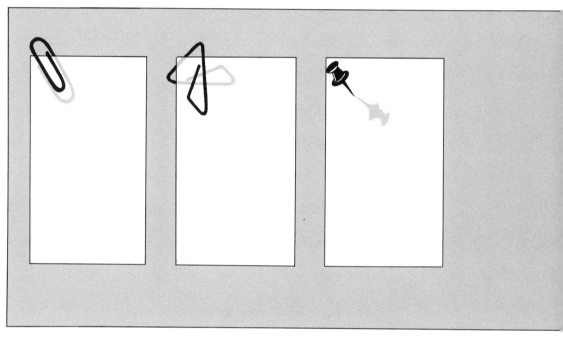

Compositions with Several Paragraphs

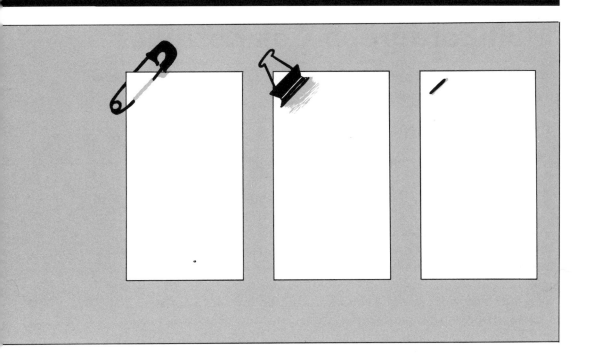

In Units 5–7, you will read and write

- **multiparagraph compositions**

- **contrastive compositions**

- **cause and effect compositions**

Multiparagraph Compositions

5.1 **We write *multiparagraph compositions* when we have too many major ideas for one paragraph.**

5.2 **Read the following composition.**

My Three Closest Friends

Like everyone else, I know all kinds of people and I'm friendly with most of them. Among all the people I've gotten to know, I have several very close friends. First I'll introduce you to my friend William. We've known one another since the first grade, when he moved in next door and was put in my class. We share secrets and many activities, like playing baseball on the same team. In William, I have a friend with whom I can relax and be myself. Another important person to me is Janet. Janet is three years older than I, and I think of her as a big sister. Janet and I used to ride the same bus to school, and sometimes she and I would sit together. In all the years I've known her, Janet has given me much useful advice and encouragement, particularly about school. Janet is one friend I know I can always depend on during good times and bad times. The third person I think is special is Tom. Tom and I are taking a photography class now, and we spend at least two evenings a week together. He's got a great eye for composition and a terrific sense of humor, and we have a lot of fun. Tom's a great friend to have around when I'm feeling sad. William, Janet, and Tom—each of them is important to me in a different way. I feel lucky to have such good friends.

5.3   Now read the same composition divided into paragraphs.

My Three Closest Friends

Like everyone else, I know all kinds of people and I'm friendly with most of them. Among all the people I've gotten to know, I have several very close friends.

First I'll introduce you to my friend William. We've known one another since the first grade, when he moved in next door and was put in my class. We share secrets and many activities, like playing baseball on the same team. In William, I have a friend with whom I can relax and be myself.

Another important person to me is Janet. Janet is three years older than I, and I think of her as a big sister. Janet and I used to ride the same bus to school, and sometimes she and I would sit together. In all the years I've known her, Janet has given me much useful advice and encouragement, particularly about school. Janet is one friend I know I can always depend on during good times and bad times.

The third person I think is special is Tom. Tom and I are taking a photography class now, and we spend at least two evenings a week together. He's got a great eye for composition and a terrific sense of humor, and we have a lot of fun. Tom's a great friend to have around when I'm feeling sad.

William, Janet, and Tom—each of them is important to me in a different way. I feel lucky to have such good friends.

5.4   The composition in 5.3 was easier to read than the composition in 5.2, wasn't it?

Why? _____

_____

_____

What was the method of organization used in the composition? (The methods are simple listing, order of importance, time order, and spatial order.)

_____

_____

5.5 **Read the unparagraphed composition below. Indicate how it could be broken into paragraphs. Mark the *beginning* of each paragraph with a *B*, and mark the *end* of each paragraph with an *E*.**

Three Places I'd Like to Visit

I've been to only a few foreign countries. Visiting those countries made me eager to do even more traveling. There are many countries that I would like to visit, but there are three special places I'd like to see above all. The first is Tahiti. I've read books and magazine articles about the South Pacific, and I've even seen a couple of films that were made there. To me it seems like heaven on earth. I can picture myself lying relaxed under a palm tree on a beautiful beach watching the sun set over a peaceful lagoon. I know this picture may not be realistic, but I'd really love to see what Tahiti is like for myself. The second place I'm longing to visit is London. There's so much to see there. I'd like to see Buckingham Palace and visit the Houses of Parliament. I'd like to see Big Ben and Tower Bridge. I especially want to see the British Museum with its historic treasures from all over the world. To me, going to London would bring to life much of the history I've studied. The third place I want to visit is Brazil. From what I've read, it seems like a very lively and exciting place. I want to lie on the beach at Copacabana. I dream of taking a boat trip up the Amazon through the jungle. I would enjoy visiting the ultramodern capital of Brasilia. Brazil offers the possibility for both adventure and relaxation. Tahiti, London, and Brazil are obviously quite different. However, each has its own attraction for me.

5.6   Now outline "Three Places I'd Like to Visit" from 5.5.

Method of Organization _____

Introduction

Central Idea _____

Body

First Paragraph

Central idea _____

Body

Conclusion _____

Second Paragraph

Central idea _____

Body

Conclusion _____

Third Paragraph

Central idea _____

Body

Conclusion _____

Conclusion

Central idea _____

5.7   Now outline your first multiparagraph composition. The topic is two important books you have read and why they are important to you. First answer the questions below.

1. Why are books important to you?

_____

2. What was the first book?

_____

3. Why was it important?

_____

4. What was the second book?

_____

5. Why was it important?

_____

6. Is there a connection between the two books?

_____

Now complete the outline.

Method of Organization <u>SIMPLE LISTING</u>

Introduction

Central idea <u>(see 1 in 5.7)</u>

_____

Other information: _____

Body

First Paragraph

Central idea <u>(see 2 in 5.7)</u>

_____

Other information (see 3 in 5.7): _____

_____

Second Paragraph

Central idea (see 4 in 5.7) _____

Other information (see 5 in 5.7): _____

_____

Conclusion (see 6 in 5.7) _____

_____

Title _____

5.8 Now write a four-paragraph composition based on your outline in 5.7.

_____

_____

_____

_____

_____

_____

_____

_____

_____

_____

_____

_____

_____

_____

5.9   Read this composition.

Things I Love to Do

My spare time is filled with a variety of activities. You might find me reading biographies or listening to country music. I might be watching baseball or college football on television. However, I can count three activities as my definite favorites.

The first is playing the guitar. I heard a famous guitarist give a concert in a big auditorium when I was a child. I begged and begged until my parents let me take lessons. I saved up to buy my own guitar. I still take lessons and sometimes write my own songs. I find playing the guitar a way both to relax and to express my inner feelings.

The activity I would choose as second best is bicycling. On weekends I often go with other bicycle club members on long rides of twenty or thirty miles. Usually we make a midway stop for lunch. Often we see a special view or landmark. In summer I've taken organized trips to the Grand Canyon and to the California wine country. For me, bicycling is a way to stay in shape and get around cheaply.

What I like third best is cooking. Mostly I bake breads and pies, but I'm beginning to cook more complete meals. I have even had several large dinner parties and served four separate courses. My specialties are whole-wheat bread and apple pie, and I have my own secret chili recipe. I like cooking for myself, and I find cooking for others a way of keeping in touch with friends.

I have many interests to keep me from being bored, but playing the guitar, bicycling, and cooking are activities that I enjoy the most. An added plus is that I can share them with others.

5.10 **Now outline "Things I Love to Do" from 5.9.**

Method of Organization _____

Introduction

Central idea _____

Other information:

Body

First Paragraph

Central idea _____

Other information:

Second Paragraph

Central idea _____

Other information:

Third Paragraph

Central idea _____

Other information:

Conclusion

Central idea _____

_____

5.11   **Now outline a multiparagraph composition. The topic is your three most enjoyable pastimes.**

Method of Organization   <u>ORDER OF IMPORTANCE</u>

Introduction

Central idea _____

Other information:

Body

First Paragraph

Central idea _____

Other information:

Second Paragraph

Central idea _____

Other information:

Third Paragraph

Central idea _____

Other information:

Conclusion

Central idea _____

Title _____

5.12 Now write a five-paragraph composition based on your outline in 5.11.

5.13 Read this composition.

Two Experiences

I had two experiences last year that helped me understand better the problem of communication between people from different countries.

While traveling to Mexico City on a bus, I became very sick. A stranger on the bus—a well-dressed, middle-aged man—helped me greatly. He personally took me off the bus, found out where the nearest doctor's office was, and accompanied me there. He helped me get the medicine the doctor prescribed and found me a hotel room. The next day, when I felt better, he came to visit me. I don't speak Spanish well, so I couldn't talk with him very much. However, even though we couldn't talk, we could communicate. I communicated my thanks for his great kindness, and he clearly communicated his kindness and concern for my health. Through this experience I learned that communication can take place without much actual language at all.

The second experience was at school. A new student came from Southeast Asia. He couldn't speak English, so he had a lot of trouble for the first few months. I tried to help him, but most of my classmates only became annoyed with him because he couldn't speak English. They had little experience with foreigners, and, after a while, they stopped trying to talk with him. I was very disappointed with my schoolmates' attitudes.

These two experiences taught me an important lesson. It is that the essential part of communication with someone from another country is really wanting to communicate.

5.14 Now outline "Two Experiences" from 5.13.

Method of Organization ___TIME ORDER_____

Introduction

Central idea _____

_____

Other information:

Body

First Paragraph

Central idea _____

_____

Other information:

Second Paragraph

Central idea _____

_____

Other information:

Conclusion

Central idea _____

_____

5.15 **Now outline a multiparagraph composition. The topic is two important events that affected your education.**

Method of Organization ___TIME ORDER___

Introduction

Central idea _____

Other information:

Body

First Paragraph

Central idea _____

Other information:

Second Paragraph

Central idea _____

Other information:

Conclusion

Central idea _____

Title _____

5.16 Now write a four-paragraph composition based on your outline in 5.15.

5.17 *FREE PRACTICE*

Write a multiparagraph composition on any subject you choose. For a method of organization, you may use simple listing, order of importance, or time order.

First outline your composition.

Method of Organization _____

Introduction

Central idea _____

Other information:

Body

First Paragraph

Central idea _____

Other information:

Second Paragraph

Central idea _____

Other information:

Conclusion

Central idea _____

Title _____

_____

5.18 **Now write your paragraph.**

_____

_____

_____

_____

_____

_____

_____

_____

_____

_____

_____

_____

_____

_____

_____

_____

_____

_____

_____

_____

_____

_____

UNIT 6

Contrastive Compositions

6.1   **When we want to compare two or more things, we write a** *contrastive composition.*

6.2   **Read this contrastive composition.**

Two Cities

Boston and San Francisco are two of the most visited American cities. Each has its own "personality" and character, which are often appreciated by people who live elsewhere.

Boston has the ethnic "flavor" typical of many cities in the East. This gives Boston the homey character of a city of neighborhoods. One ethnic group whose presence is felt is the Irish, who have become important in the politics of the city and state, of whom President John F. Kennedy is an example. The many universities in and around the city make Boston a leading center for higher education. Boston is also a high-tech center, with many white-collar workers in fields related to the computer industry. Its homey and high-tech sides make Boston a diverse city.

San Francisco lies on the West Coast, a continent away from Boston. Like Boston, it has ethnic areas, including the world-famous Chinatown. Unlike Boston, however, the city did not follow the typical pattern of growing through a steady influx of immigrants. San Francisco grew dramatically as a result of being near the gold fields, which were the goal of the famous gold rush of 1849. Yet many visitors feel San Francisco is a big city that has kept a small-city feel. Some physical features help make San Francisco unique among American cities. It is built on steep hills, which give many dramatic views. Another famous area of the city that provides a lovely panorama is the wharf, where one can shop or dine on a wide variety of fish. A center of finance in the western United States, San

Francisco also boasts a rich cultural life. It was the birthplace of many avant-garde movements, from the Beatniks of the 1950s and the Flower Children of the 1960s to the sexual liberation movements of the 1970s and 1980s. San Francisco always seems to be ahead of its time.

These cities show the diversity of American urban areas. They prove the variety possible within and between cities.

6.3 Now outline the ideas from "Two Cities" in 6.2.

Introduction _____

_____

Body

Boston

Introduction/Central idea

Body

Conclusion

San Francisco

Introduction/Central idea

Body

Conclusion

Conclusion _____

_____

6.4   Now outline your own contrastive composition about two places you know well.

Introduction _____

_____

_____

_____

Body

_____ *(first place)*

Introduction/Central idea

Body

Conclusion

_____ *(second place)*

Introduction/Central idea

Body

Conclusion

Conclusion _____

_____

_____

_____

Title _____

6.5 **Now write a contrastive composition based on your outline in 6.4.**

6.6   **Now read another contrastive composition.**

The Same Person?

The other day, I ran into someone I hadn't seen for many years. I couldn't believe the change in him. In fact, he didn't even seem like the same person.

When I first knew Bill, back in college, he was one of the most easygoing, carefree people I had ever met. He was always ready to have a party. He thought nothing of going out for pizza at three o'clock in the morning or driving 50 miles to see an old movie he really liked. Bill and I were in the same dormitory in college, and life was never dull when he was around. With him there was one wild adventure after another. One time we went to a garage sale and bought old suits from the 1930s. They looked like gangster suits, with broad, loud stripes and big lapels. We wore the suits for an entire Memorial Day weekend. By the end of the weekend, we had cut off the sleeves of the jackets and the legs of the pants above the knees and were actually going swimming in them. Sometimes I wonder how we ever managed to study for our exams.

Last weekend I was in Houston on business, and I ran into Bill in the bar at the hotel. At first, I wasn't even sure it was he. Was this short-haired, conservatively dressed businessman really the same person? I wasn't really sure until I approached him, but it indeed was Bill. Now he works for a bank. He talked most of the evening about his job, his new car, and his house. How he had changed! Back when we were in college, the last thing Bill cared about were possessions. Now they seemed to be his major obsession. Although I have changed quite a bit myself, somehow I never imagined Bill changing so much. My image of him remained the one I had formed at the time when we were college students together.

I suppose it's foolish to expect people to remain the same, especially when I have changed so much myself. But I must say that I enjoyed the old Bill much more than the new Bill. Maybe he felt the same way about me.

6.7   Now outline "The Same Person?" in 6.6.

Introduction _____

_____

Body

Bill at college

Introduction/Central idea

Body

Conclusion

Bill, last weekend

Introduction/Central idea

Body

Conclusion

Conclusion _____

_____

6.8 **Now outline your own composition about the changes you have seen in a person. These differences can be because of the passage of time, or because you met the person in a different situation, or because you got to know the person better.**

Introduction _____

_____

Body

First impression of the person _____

_____

Introduction/Central idea

Body

Conclusion

Second impression of the person _____

_____

Introduction/Central idea

Body

Conclusion

Conclusion _____

_____

_____

Title _____

6.9   Now write a composition based on your outline in 6.8.

6.10 **Now read a contrastive composition that tells about the physical changes in a place.**

Two Big Changes

When I revisited southern California after about forty years, I found that many changes had taken place. The biggest change was in the landscape. The change that I noticed second was in the pace of life.

Forty years ago the land around Los Angeles was mostly farms and open spaces. It took only a few minutes to drive out of the city and feel one was in the country. On returning to the city forty years later, I was immediately struck by the amount of building that had taken place. Former farmland was now residential communities. Barren canyons were filled with schools, shops, and houses. Near-desert areas were filled with large industrial parks. This was the most dramatic change I noticed.

The second biggest change seemed to be in the pace of life. When I first went to Los Angeles, it seemed a relaxed and easygoing community where time was less important than comfort. On the other hand, today's Los Angeles is as active and exciting as any city in the country. Indeed, it seems as hectic as any other city.

I guess any place changes in forty years. I know I found many changes in Los Angeles, and some of them were disappointing. Forty years from now, I suppose it will be just as different from today as today seems from forty years ago.

6.11 **Now outline "Two Big Changes" from 6.10.**

Introduction _____

_____

_____

_____

Body

Landscape

Introduction/Central idea

Body

Conclusion

Pace of life

Introduction/Central idea

Body

Conclusion

Conclusion _____

_____

_____

_____

_____

6.12 **Now outline your own contrastive composition on the changes you have seen in a place over time. It may be a short period of time or a longer period of time.**

Introduction _____

_____

Body

First change = _____

Introduction/Central idea

Body

Conclusion

Second change = _____

Introduction/Central idea

Body

Conclusion

Third change = _____

Introduction/Central idea

Body

Conclusion

Conclusion _____

_____

Title _____

6.13   Now write a composition based on your outline in 6.12.

6.14 Read this contrastive composition about two famous American authors.

Hemingway and Fitzgerald

After World War I, a new generation of American writers emerged. They were called the lost generation, and many of them reached artistic maturity in Paris in the period between the two wars. Among these writers, two men are undoubtedly the most well known, Ernest Hemingway and F. Scott Fitzgerald. These two writers, from different backgrounds and with different literary sensibilities, were certainly the foremost writers of their generation.

Ernest Hemingway was born and brought up in Oak Park, a suburb of Chicago. His father was a doctor, and his upbringing was very conventional. Aside from writing, which he began doing in high school, his father's hobbies of hunting and fishing were to be an important influence on his life and his life's work. He worked as a newspaper reporter from right after high school until he joined the volunteer ambulance drivers corps in World War I. He was injured in Italy and returned to the United States where, after he had recovered, he again became a reporter. His background as a reporter had a big effect on his writing style, which has been described as "spartan." He used short, direct sentences, eliminating much of the "flowery" language that had until then been considered good writing style. He returned to Europe as a newspaper reporter after the war and began his serious writing career there. In 1926, he published his first highly acclaimed novel, *The Sun Also Rises*. He became a celebrity for both his writing and his life-style. Throughout his life he devoted large amounts of time to his interests in big-game hunting, sport fishing, and bullfighting. He incorporated many themes from these pastimes into his novels. In failing health, he took his own life in 1961.

F. Scott Fitzgerald was born to an aristocratic, but impoverished family, in 1896. He first achieved prominence at Yale University, where he was a literary figure until he was expelled. He joined the army during World War I, but the end of the war saw him as a poorly paid office worker in New York. He kept writing and in 1920 achieved fame for his first popular novel, *This Side of Paradise*. This book described the fun-seeking young generation of the postwar period. He and his wife, Zelda, soon became social and literary figures of prominence in New York, so much so that they began to feel suffocated. They left for Europe in 1924 to escape this "gilded" prison. During the 1930s, Fitzgerald continued to write successfully, but his domestic life began to break up. His wife became mentally ill, and he became an alcoholic. His last years were spent in Hollywood, where he was at work on one of his most powerful books when he died of a heart attack at the age of forty-four.

Both Hemingway and Fitzgerald had their unique views of the world and of human nature. Hemingway's view was at the same time robust, masculine, and sensitive. Fitzgerald's view probed society and its values. Both improve our understanding of the human condition.

6.15 **Now outline "Hemingway and Fitzgerald" from 6.14.**

Introduction _____

_____

_____

Body

Hemingway

Introduction

Body

Conclusion

Fitzgerald

Introduction

Body

Conclusion

Conclusion _____

_____

_____

6.16 **Now write an outline for a contrastive composition. The theme can be one of the following:**

- two different, but related, books you've read
- two different, but related, movies you've seen
- two different cars of the same type
- two different musicians or bands

Introduction _____

_____

_____

Body

1st item: _____

Introduction

Body

Conclusion

2nd item: _____

Introduction

Body

Conclusion

Conclusion _____

_____

_____

Title _____

_____

6.17 Now write a composition based on your outline in 6.16.

6.18 *FREE PRACTICE*

Now write a contrastive composition that shows the difference between any two people or things you'd like to compare.

First outline your composition.

Introduction _____

_____

Body

1st item: _____

Introduction

Body

Conclusion

2nd item: _____

Introduction

Body

Conclusion

Conclusion _____

_____

Title _____

6.19   Now write the composition.

_____

_____

_____

_____

_____

_____

_____

_____

_____

_____

_____

_____

_____

_____

_____

_____

_____

_____

_____

_____

_____

_____

_____

_____

UNIT 7

Cause and Effect Compositions

7.1 We write *cause and effect compositions* when we want to explain what happened and why it happened.

7.2 Read the following cause and effect composition. As you read, notice that the first paragraph of the body gives information about "causes"—what the writer wanted in a career. The second paragraph of the body gives information about "effects"—what the writer decided about her career choice.

Choosing My Career

My decision to become a nurse was based on several well-thought-out reasons. Some of my reasons had to do with personal goals. Other reasons had to do with my view of society and where I want to fit into society.

During my last year in high school, I had several long conversations with my parents about what to do after I graduated. Through these talks, I was able to clarify my career goals. I wanted a job with good pay and good status. These were not my only goals. I also wanted a job that would help people in a practical way, a job that could make people's lives better.

Taking these reasons into consideration, I was able to narrow down my choices to two jobs. The first was teaching. I have always liked children, and I like teaching people to do things. A teacher also makes a decent living and gets a fair amount of respect if he or she does her job well. I would also be able to help people as a teacher. The second choice was nursing. Nursing met all my criteria for a job. In addition, it is a job I could continue to do periodically or part-time if I decided to have children. Finally, I decided on nursing as a career since it offered me a good-paying, respected position with a lot of flexibility.

I'm now in my last year of nursing school, and I'm looking forward to starting my professional life. I feel certain I made the right choice.

7.3   Now outline "Choosing My Career" from 7.2.

Introduction _____

_____

Body

Cause

Introduction

Body

Conclusion

Effect

Introduction

Body

Conclusion

Conclusion _____

_____

_____

7.4 Write an outline for a composition on one of the following:

- choosing a college major—what and why
- choosing your career—what and why

Introduction _____

_____

Body

Cause

Introduction

Body

Conclusion

Effect

Introduction

Body

Conclusion

Conclusion _____

_____

Title _____

7.5   Now write a composition based on your outline in 7.4.

_____

_____

_____

_____

_____

_____

_____

_____

_____

_____

_____

_____

_____

_____

_____

_____

_____

_____

_____

_____

_____

_____

_____

7.6 Now read another cause and effect composition. Like the composition in 7.2, the first paragraph in the body gives information about the cause, and the second paragraph in the body gives information about the effect.

The "Supermarketing" of America

Drive through any American city or suburb, and you will see large spaces where huge stores are grouped together, sometimes even under one roof. The sight of such large stores would have been unusual for our grandparents, who shopped in small, neighborhood stores. These shopping areas reflect some major changes in American society.

The construction of new supermarkets and shopping centers has been continuing over the past forty years. Supermarkets continue to appear because they offer the consumer a wide choice of products in one place—anything from food to small appliances. Because of the large amount of goods sold, supermarkets can offer lower prices than smaller neighborhood stores can. The convenience and value of large stores and shopping areas have made them an essential part of the way Americans shop.

With the rise of supermarkets and shopping centers, American society has experienced some changes. Most obviously, many small neighborhood stores have disappeared, driven out of business by the larger stores. Now Americans use cars even more in order to get to and carry products from the shopping centers, which are typically located farther from many homes. Another change is perhaps the most subtle and least easy to describe. Americans are now more isolated. In the neighborhood store, the owner knew about the customers and their families. People in the neighborhood could gather and talk there. Now Americans shop in huge spaces, where no one knows anyone else. Supermarkets have made shopping more impersonal.

It is clear that the number of supermarkets and large shopping areas is still increasing. The pattern of "bigger is better" will probably continue into the future.

7.7   Now outline "The 'Supermarketing' of America" from 7.6.

Introduction _____

_____

Body

Cause

Introduction

Body

Conclusion

Effect

Introduction

Body

Conclusion

Conclusion _____

_____

7.8   Now write your outline for a cause and effect composition on one of the following:

- the reasons for a change in the job market and what it may mean for the future
- the reasons for a change in a company or school policy and what it may mean for the future

Introduction _____

_____

Body

Cause

Introduction

Body

Conclusion

Effect

Introduction

Body

Conclusion

Conclusion _____

_____

Title _____

_____

7.9 Now write a cause and effect composition based on your outline in 7.8.

_____

_____

_____

_____

_____

_____

_____

_____

_____

_____

_____

_____

_____

_____

_____

_____

_____

_____

_____

_____

_____

7.10   Now read this cause and effect composition. It is different from the two you have just read. In this composition, the introduction explains the effect, and each paragraph in the body explains a cause or causes.

The Growth of America

In 1800 the United States was a small country. The population was a mere 2,300,000. Most of the states bordered the Atlantic Ocean. Fifty years later, in 1850, the picture was considerably different. The country had a population of 23,000,000 and stretched from the Atlantic to the Pacific and from the Rio Grande up to the 49th parallel. There were several reasons for America's fifty years of explosive growth.

The first quantum leap in America's physical expansion was in 1803, when President Jefferson bought a huge area of land along the Mississippi river basin, called the Louisiana Purchase, from France. Thus, in one move, he doubled the size of the continental United States. In 1819, a treaty with Spain added the peninsula of Florida to the United States. Texas was annexed in 1845, a move that ultimately led to even greater expansion. In 1846, with the settlement of the Oregon dispute, Great Britain recognized the 49th parallel as America's northwest border with Canada, and thus the area of the present-day states of Oregon, Washington, and Utah was added to the Union. Upon the annexation of Texas, Mexico and the United States began to fight a war. After America's military victory in 1848, Mexico was forced to sell a piece of land called the Mexican Cession, which included California, Nevada, and Arizona, as well as parts of Colorado and New Mexico. The final piece of the continental United States fell into place with the Gadsden Purchase in 1853, when the U.S. bought a strip of contested land in the Southwest from Mexico.

The population growth in the United States was accounted for by two factors: family size and immigration. Families with five or six children were not uncommon. Large families were actually an economic advantage at a time when most families lived and worked on farms. The second reason was the huge amount of immigration that took place. Between 1841 and 1850 alone, there were over 1,700,000 immigrants to the United States. They came mostly from Europe, primarily from Germany, Ireland, Great Britain, and France.

As a result of the active expansionist policies of several successive presidential administrations and the quadrupling of the population, America, in fifty short years, became the country we recognize today.

7.11   Now outline "The Growth of America" from 7.10.

Introduction _____

_____

Body

Physical expansion

Population

Conclusion _____

_____

7.12 Now outline your own composition on one of the following themes:

- two or three factors that led to a change in your life-style
- two or three factors that caused you to change your ideas about something

Introduction _____

_____

Body

1st factor _____

_____

_____

_____

2nd factor _____

_____

_____

_____

3rd factor _____

_____

_____

_____

Conclusion _____

_____

_____

Title _____

7.13   Now write a composition based on your outline in 7.12.

7.14 Now read this final cause and effect composition. Its outline is different from the others you have studied. In this composition, each paragraph in the body explains a cause and an effect that take place in a larger process.

A Successful Venture

Several years ago, my company, which is a travel business, was looking for ways to expand. We were particularly interested in Southeast Asia, but had no experience doing business in that area. When we decided to expand, the first thing we did was assign one of our managers to do a feasibility study. The study was an integral part of the successful expansion strategy we developed.

The first step the manager took was to visit the places on our list: Hong Kong, Thailand, Burma, Malaysia, Indonesia, and Brunei. In each country he visited the sights that would interest our customers and checked carefully on the facilities available for tourists. In this way, he was quickly able to eliminate Burma and Brunei as practical areas for expansion.

As the next step, he visited the tourism ministries of the remaining four places. At each ministry, he asked what kind of help was available in promoting tourism. This enabled him to save a lot of time on research.

After that he estimated the cost and potential profit of expanding into each country. His findings were that the best order of development, from the point of view of costs and potential profit, was Thailand, Hong Kong, Malaysia, and Indonesia. These findings were presented to our board, and it was decided that it would be too expensive to develop our business in all these areas at once. We therefore decided to enter the countries one by one in the order suggested in the manager's report.

Our manager did a very thorough job. He got the information necessary and did so in an efficient manner. Through his well-thought-out approach, we have been able to construct a long-term strategy for profitably expanding our business.

7.15   Now outline "A Successful Venture" from 7.14.

Introduction _____

_____

Body

The 1st step

Cause

Effect

The 2nd step

Cause

Effect

The 3rd step

Cause

Effect

Conclusion _____

_____

_____

7.16   Now outline your own cause and effect composition on one of the following themes:

- the steps you took or will take in choosing a place to live
- the steps you took or will take in choosing a college
- the steps you took or will take in making any complicated decision

Introduction _____

_____

Body

The 1st step

Cause

Effect

The 2nd step

Cause

Effect

The 3rd step

Cause

Effect

Conclusion _____

_____

Title _____

7.17   Now write a composition based on your outline in 7.16.

_____

_____

_____

_____

_____

_____

_____

_____

_____

_____

_____

_____

_____

_____

_____

_____

_____

_____

_____

_____

7.18   *FREE PRACTICE*

Outline and write a cause and effect composition on any topic you like.

First prepare an outline.

Introduction _____

_____

Body

Conclusion _____

_____

Title _____

7.19 **Now write your composition.**